Reptiles

Elizabeth Nonweiler

raintree

grass snake

night adder

banded sea krait

coast garter snake

beaded lizard

whiptail lizard

river cooter

pond terrapin

black caiman

white caiman

Nile crocodile

mugger crocodile

Interesting facts about the pictures

page 2: The **grass snake** is the largest reptile in the United Kingdom. It likes to bask in the sun in summer, but when it is cold, it goes underground to keep warm. It is not poisonous.

page 3: The **night adder** lives in Africa and comes out at day or night. If you disturb one it will hiss, puff up, rise off the ground in a coil and swipe at you and then try to glide away quickly.

page 4: **Banded sea kraits** live in warm oceans and swim to the surface to breathe. They hunt for fish in coral reefs, poison them to stop them moving and then eat them.

page 5: **Coast garter snakes** live near the Pacific Ocean in the United States. They eat small animals, but sometimes hawks or racoons try to eat them. Then they slither into water to get away.

page 6: The **beaded lizard** has scales like beads. It lives in Mexico and Guatemala. It eats eggs and small animals. If you prod one, it might poison you, but its poison is good in medicines.

page 7: **Whiptail lizards** live in hot dry parts of North America. They have very long tails and can move fast to hide under rocks when they are in danger.

page 8: **River cooters** are large turtles that live in rivers, lakes and marshes in North America. They enjoy lying on rocks in the sun, but they sleep in the water. They lay their eggs on land.

page 9: **Pond terrapins** are small turtles that live near water in Europe, Asia and North Africa. They like to lay their eggs in the same place every year. This is a European terrapin.

page 10: **Black caimans** live in the rainforest of South America. They are about four metres long. Baby black caimans eat small fish and insects, but adults eat animals as big as horses.

page 11: **White caimans** are smaller than black caimans. They live in South America and eat insects, fish and snails. Mother caimans take care of each other's babies after they hatch.

page 12: The **Nile crocodile** lives in Africa and takes its name from the River Nile. It can be more than five metres long. It has powerful jaws and will kill and eat almost any other animal.

page 13: The **mugger crocodile** lives in rivers, swamps and marshes in India and Pakistan. It hides in murky waters until it sees an animal to eat and then it launches an attack.

Letter-sound correspondences

Level 2 books cover the following letter-sound correspondences.
Letter-sound correspondences highlighted in green can be found in this book.

<u>a</u>nt	<u>b</u>ig	<u>c</u>at	<u>d</u>og	<u>e</u>gg	**f**ish	<u>g</u>et	**h**ot	<u>i</u>t
jet	<u>k</u>ey	<u>l</u>et	<u>m</u>an	<u>n</u>ut	<u>o</u>ff	<u>p</u>an	**qu**een	<u>r</u>un
<u>s</u>un	<u>t</u>ap	<u>u</u>p	<u>v</u>an	**w**et	bo**x**	**y**es	zoo	
du<u>ck</u>	fi<u>**sh**</u>	<u>**ch**</u>ips	si<u>**ng**</u>	**thin** **this**	k<u>ee</u>p	l<u>oo</u>k m<u>oo</u>n	<u>ar</u>t	c<u>or</u>n

s<u>**ay**</u>	b<u>**oy**</u>	r<u>ai</u>n	<u>**oi**</u>l	b<u>oa</u>t	<u>ea</u>t	p<u>ie</u>	h<u>igh</u>
m<u>a</u>k<u>e</u>	th<u>**ese**</u>	l<u>i</u>k<u>e</u>	n<u>o</u>t<u>e</u>	fl<u>**ute**</u> t<u>**ube**</u>	<u>**ou**</u>t	s<u>**aw**</u>	<u>**au**</u>thor
h<u>er</u>	b<u>ir</u>d	t<u>ur</u>n	<u>**air**</u>port	fl<u>**ew**</u> st<u>**ew**</u>	bl<u>**ue**</u> c<u>**ue**</u>	**ph**one	<u>wh</u>en